This Prayer Book
Belongs To:

_____

My Yearly Goals

Date: _____

Scripture Memory

Bible Study Goals

Verse of the Year

My Prayers

Date: _____

My Family	My Friends
Those In Need	**Myself**

Date: _____

My Prayers

_____
_____
_____
_____

My Prayers For Others

_____
_____
_____
_____

Thankful For

_____
_____
_____

Weekly Bible Study Schedule

Date: _____

Sunday	Monday	Tuesday
Wednesday	Thursday	Friday

Saturday	Notes

My Daily Prayers

Date: _____

People to Pray For

I'm Grateful For

Prayer For Today

My Daily Prayers

Date: _____

People to Pray For

I'm Grateful For

Prayer For Today

My Daily Prayers

Date:_____

People to Pray For

I'm Grateful For

Prayer For Today

My Daily Prayers

Date: _____

People to Pray For

I'm Grateful For

Prayer For Today

My Daily Prayers

Date:_____

People to Pray For

I'm Grateful For

Prayer For Today

My Daily Prayers

Date: _____

People to Pray For

I'm Grateful For

Prayer For Today

My Daily Prayers

Date: _____

People to Pray For

I'm Grateful For

Prayer For Today

Weekly Bible Study Schedule

Date: _____

Sunday	Monday	Tuesday

Wednesday	Thursday	Friday

Saturday	Notes

My Daily Prayers

Date: _____

People to Pray For

I'm Grateful For

Prayer For Today

My Daily Prayers

Date: _____

People to Pray For

I'm Grateful For

Prayer For Today

My Daily Prayers

Date: _____

People to Pray For

I'm Grateful For

Prayer For Today

My Daily Prayers

Date: _____

People to Pray For

I'm Grateful For

Prayer For Today

My Daily Prayers

Date: _____

People to Pray For

I'm Grateful For

Prayer For Today

My Daily Prayers

Date: _____

People to Pray For

I'm Grateful For

Prayer For Today

My Daily Prayers

Date:_____

People to Pray For

I'm Grateful For

Prayer For Today

Weekly Bible Study Schedule

Date: _____

Sunday	Monday	Tuesday

Wednesday	Thursday	Friday

Saturday	Notes

My Daily Prayers

Date: _____

People to Pray For

I'm Grateful For

Prayer For Today

My Daily Prayers

Date: _____

People to Pray For

I'm Grateful For

Prayer For Today

My Daily Prayers

Date:_____

People to Pray For

I'm Grateful For

Prayer For Today

My Daily Prayers

Date: _____

People to Pray For

I'm Grateful For

Prayer For Today

My Daily Prayers

Date:_____

People to Pray For

I'm Grateful For

Prayer For Today

My Daily Prayers

Date: _____

People to Pray For

I'm Grateful For

Prayer For Today

My Daily Prayers

Date:_____

People to Pray For

I'm Grateful For

Prayer For Today

Weekly Bible Study Schedule

Date: _____

Sunday	Monday	Tuesday

Wednesday	Thursday	Friday

Saturday	Notes

My Daily Prayers

Date: _____

People to Pray For

I'm Grateful For

Prayer For Today

My Daily Prayers

Date: _____

People to Pray For

I'm Grateful For

Prayer For Today

My Daily Prayers

Date: _____

People to Pray For

I'm Grateful For

Prayer For Today

My Daily Prayers

Date: _____

People to Pray For

I'm Grateful For

Prayer For Today

My Daily Prayers

Date: _____

People to Pray For

I'm Grateful For

Prayer For Today

My Daily Prayers

Date: _____

People to Pray For

I'm Grateful For

Prayer For Today

My Daily Prayers

Date: _____

People to Pray For

I'm Grateful For

Prayer For Today

Weekly Bible Study Schedule

Date: _____

Sunday	Monday	Tuesday

Wednesday	Thursday	Friday

Saturday	Notes

My Daily Prayers

Date: _____

People to Pray For

I'm Grateful For

Prayer For Today

My Daily Prayers

Date: _____

People to Pray For

I'm Grateful For

Prayer For Today

My Daily Prayers

Date:_____

People to Pray For

I'm Grateful For

Prayer For Today

My Daily Prayers

Date: _____

People to Pray For

I'm Grateful For

Prayer For Today

My Daily Prayers

Date: _____

People to Pray For

I'm Grateful For

Prayer For Today

My Daily Prayers

Date: _____

People to Pray For

I'm Grateful For

Prayer For Today

My Daily Prayers

Date:_____

People to Pray For

I'm Grateful For

Prayer For Today

Weekly Bible Study Schedule

Date: _____

Sunday	Monday	Tuesday

Wednesday	Thursday	Friday

Saturday	Notes

My Daily Prayers

Date:_____

People to Pray For

I'm Grateful For

Prayer For Today

My Daily Prayers

Date: _____

People to Pray For

I'm Grateful For

Prayer For Today

My Daily Prayers

Date: _____

People to Pray For

I'm Grateful For

Prayer For Today

My Daily Prayers

Date: _____

People to Pray For

I'm Grateful For

Prayer For Today

My Daily Prayers

Date: _____

People to Pray For

I'm Grateful For

Prayer For Today

My Daily Prayers

Date: _____

People to Pray For

I'm Grateful For

Prayer For Today

My Daily Prayers

Date: _____

People to Pray For

I'm Grateful For

Prayer For Today

Weekly Bible Study Schedule

Date: _____

Sunday	Monday	Tuesday
Wednesday	Thursday	Friday

Saturday	Notes

My Daily Prayers

Date: _____

People to Pray For

I'm Grateful For

Prayer For Today

My Daily Prayers

Date: _____

People to Pray For

I'm Grateful For

Prayer For Today

My Daily Prayers

Date: _____

People to Pray For

I'm Grateful For

Prayer For Today

My Daily Prayers

Date: _____

People to Pray For

I'm Grateful For

Prayer For Today

My Daily Prayers

Date: _____

People to Pray For

I'm Grateful For

Prayer For Today

My Daily Prayers

Date: _____

People to Pray For

I'm Grateful For

Prayer For Today

My Daily Prayers

Date: _____

People to Pray For

I'm Grateful For

Prayer For Today

Weekly Bible Study Schedule

Date: _____

Sunday	Monday	Tuesday

Wednesday	Thursday	Friday

Saturday	Notes

My Daily Prayers

Date: _____

People to Pray For

I'm Grateful For

Prayer For Today

My Daily Prayers

Date: _____

People to Pray For

I'm Grateful For

Prayer For Today

My Daily Prayers

Date: _____

People to Pray For

I'm Grateful For

Prayer For Today

My Daily Prayers

Date: _____

People to Pray For

I'm Grateful For

Prayer For Today

My Daily Prayers

Date:_____

People to Pray For

I'm Grateful For

Prayer For Today

My Daily Prayers

Date: _____

People to Pray For

I'm Grateful For

Prayer For Today

My Daily Prayers

Date: _____

People to Pray For

I'm Grateful For

Prayer For Today

Weekly Bible Study Schedule

Date: _____

Sunday	Monday	Tuesday

Wednesday	Thursday	Friday

Saturday	Notes

My Daily Prayers

Date: _____

People to Pray For

I'm Grateful For

Prayer For Today

My Daily Prayers

Date: _____

People to Pray For

I'm Grateful For

Prayer For Today

My Daily Prayers

Date: _____

People to Pray For

I'm Grateful For

Prayer For Today

My Daily Prayers

Date: _____

People to Pray For

I'm Grateful For

Prayer For Today

My Daily Prayers

Date: _____

People to Pray For

I'm Grateful For

Prayer For Today

My Daily Prayers

Date: _____

People to Pray For

I'm Grateful For

Prayer For Today

My Daily Prayers

Date:_____

People to Pray For

I'm Grateful For

Prayer For Today

Weekly Bible Study Schedule

Date: _____

Sunday	Monday	Tuesday

Wednesday	Thursday	Friday

Saturday	Notes

My Daily Prayers

Date: _____

People to Pray For

I'm Grateful For

Prayer For Today

My Daily Prayers

Date: _____

People to Pray For

I'm Grateful For

Prayer For Today

My Daily Prayers

Date:_____

People to Pray For

I'm Grateful For

Prayer For Today

My Daily Prayers

Date: _____

People to Pray For

I'm Grateful For

Prayer For Today

My Daily Prayers

Date: _____

People to Pray For

I'm Grateful For

Prayer For Today

My Daily Prayers

Date: _____

People to Pray For

I'm Grateful For

Prayer For Today

My Daily Prayers

Date: _____

People to Pray For

I'm Grateful For

Prayer For Today

Weekly Bible Study Schedule

Date: _____

Sunday	Monday	Tuesday

Wednesday	Thursday	Friday

Saturday	Notes

My Daily Prayers

Date: _____

People to Pray For

I'm Grateful For

Prayer For Today

My Daily Prayers

Date: _____

People to Pray For

I'm Grateful For

Prayer For Today

My Daily Prayers

Date: _____

People to Pray For

I'm Grateful For

Prayer For Today

My Daily Prayers

Date: _____

People to Pray For

I'm Grateful For

Prayer For Today

My Daily Prayers

Date: _____

People to Pray For

I'm Grateful For

Prayer For Today

My Daily Prayers

Date: _____

People to Pray For

I'm Grateful For

Prayer For Today

My Daily Prayers

Date: _____

People to Pray For

I'm Grateful For

Prayer For Today

Weekly Bible Study Schedule

Date: _____

Sunday	Monday	Tuesday

Wednesday	Thursday	Friday

Saturday	Notes

My Daily Prayers

Date: _____

People to Pray For

I'm Grateful For

Prayer For Today

My Daily Prayers

Date: _____

People to Pray For

I'm Grateful For

Prayer For Today

My Daily Prayers

Date: _____

People to Pray For

I'm Grateful For

Prayer For Today

My Daily Prayers

Date: _____

People to Pray For

I'm Grateful For

Prayer For Today

My Daily Prayers

Date: _____

People to Pray For

I'm Grateful For

Prayer For Today

My Daily Prayers

Date: _____

People to Pray For

I'm Grateful For

Prayer For Today

My Daily Prayers

Date: _____

People to Pray For

I'm Grateful For

Prayer For Today

Weekly Bible Study Schedule

Date: _____

Sunday	Monday	Tuesday

Wednesday	Thursday	Friday

Saturday	Notes

My Daily Prayers

Date: _____

People to Pray For

I'm Grateful For

Prayer For Today

My Daily Prayers

Date: _____

People to Pray For

I'm Grateful For

Prayer For Today

My Daily Prayers

Date: _____

People to Pray For

I'm Grateful For

Prayer For Today

My Daily Prayers

Date: _____

People to Pray For

I'm Grateful For

Prayer For Today

My Daily Prayers

Date: _____

People to Pray For

I'm Grateful For

Prayer For Today

My Daily Prayers

Date: _____

People to Pray For

I'm Grateful For

Prayer For Today

My Daily Prayers

Date: _____

People to Pray For

I'm Grateful For

Prayer For Today

Weekly Bible Study Schedule

Date: _____

Sunday	Monday	Tuesday

Wednesday	Thursday	Friday

Saturday	Notes

My Daily Prayers

Date: _____

People to Pray For

I'm Grateful For

Prayer For Today

My Daily Prayers

Date: _____

People to Pray For

I'm Grateful For

Prayer For Today

My Daily Prayers

Date: _____

People to Pray For

I'm Grateful For

Prayer For Today

My Daily Prayers

Date: _____

People to Pray For

I'm Grateful For

Prayer For Today

My Daily Prayers

Date: _____

People to Pray For

I'm Grateful For

Prayer For Today

My Daily Prayers

Date: _____

People to Pray For

I'm Grateful For

Prayer For Today

My Daily Prayers

Date: _____

People to Pray For

I'm Grateful For

Prayer For Today

Weekly Bible Study Schedule

Date: _____

Sunday	Monday	Tuesday

Wednesday	Thursday	Friday

Saturday	Notes

My Daily Prayers

Date:_____

People to Pray For

I'm Grateful For

Prayer For Today

My Daily Prayers

Date: _____

People to Pray For

I'm Grateful For

Prayer For Today

My Daily Prayers

Date: _____

People to Pray For

I'm Grateful For

Prayer For Today

My Daily Prayers

Date: _____

People to Pray For

I'm Grateful For

Prayer For Today

My Daily Prayers

Date: _____

People to Pray For

I'm Grateful For

Prayer For Today

My Daily Prayers

Date:_____

People to Pray For

I'm Grateful For

Prayer For Today

My Daily Prayers

Date: _____

People to Pray For

I'm Grateful For

Prayer For Today

Weekly Bible Study Schedule

Date: _____

Sunday	Monday	Tuesday

Wednesday	Thursday	Friday

Saturday	Notes

My Daily Prayers

Date: _____

People to Pray For

I'm Grateful For

Prayer For Today

My Daily Prayers

Date: _____

People to Pray For

I'm Grateful For

Prayer For Today

My Daily Prayers

Date: _____

People to Pray For

I'm Grateful For

Prayer For Today

My Daily Prayers

Date: _____

People to Pray For

I'm Grateful For

Prayer For Today

My Daily Prayers

Date:_____

People to Pray For

I'm Grateful For

Prayer For Today

My Daily Prayers

Date:_____

People to Pray For

I'm Grateful For

Prayer For Today

My Daily Prayers

Date: _____

People to Pray For

I'm Grateful For

Prayer For Today

Reflection Notes

Date: _____

_____

_____

_____

_____

_____

_____

_____

_____

_____

_____

_____

_____

_____

Reflection Notes

Date: _____

_____

_____

_____

_____

_____

_____

_____

_____

_____

_____

_____

_____

_____

Reflection Notes

Date: _____

_____
_____
_____
_____
_____
_____
_____
_____
_____
_____
_____
_____
_____
_____

Reflection Notes

Date: _____

_____

_____

_____

_____

_____

_____

_____

_____

_____

_____

_____

_____

_____

Reflection Notes

Date: _____

_____

_____

_____

_____

_____

_____

_____

_____

_____

_____

_____

_____

_____

Reflection Notes

Date: _____

_____

_____

_____

_____

_____

_____

_____

_____

_____

_____

_____

_____

_____

Reflection Notes

Date: _____

_____

_____

_____

_____

_____

_____

_____

_____

_____

_____

_____

_____

_____

Reflection Notes

Date: _____

_____

_____

_____

_____

_____

_____

_____

_____

_____

_____

_____

_____

_____

Reflection Notes

Date: _____

_____

_____

_____

_____

_____

_____

_____

_____

_____

_____

_____

_____

_____

Reflection Notes

Date: _____

_____

_____

_____

_____

_____

_____

_____

_____

_____

_____

_____

_____

_____

_____

_____

Reflection Notes

Date: _____

Reflection Notes

Date: _____

_____

_____

_____

_____

_____

_____

_____

_____

_____

_____

_____

_____

_____

Reflection Notes

Date: _____

_____

_____

_____

_____

_____

_____

_____

_____

_____

_____

_____

_____

_____

_____

Reflection Notes

Date: _____

_____

_____

_____

_____

_____

_____

_____

_____

_____

_____

_____

_____

_____

_____

Reflection Notes

Date:_____

_____

_____

_____

_____

_____

_____

_____

_____

_____

_____

_____

_____

_____

Reflection Notes

Date: _____

_____

_____

_____

_____

_____

_____

_____

_____

_____

_____

_____

_____

_____

Reflection Notes

Date: _____

_____

_____

_____

_____

_____

_____

_____

_____

_____

_____

_____

_____

_____

_____

Reflection Notes

Date: _____

_____

_____

_____

_____

_____

_____

_____

_____

_____

_____

_____

_____

_____

_____

Reflection Notes

Date: _____

_____
_____
_____
_____
_____
_____
_____
_____
_____
_____
_____
_____
_____
_____

Reflection Notes

Date: _____

_____

_____

_____

_____

_____

_____

_____

_____

_____

_____

_____

_____

_____

_____

_____

Reflection Notes

Date: _____

_____

_____

_____

_____

_____

_____

_____

_____

_____

_____

_____

_____

_____

Reflection Notes

Date: _____

_____

_____

_____

_____

_____

_____

_____

_____

_____

_____

_____

_____

_____

Reflection Notes

Date: _____

_____

_____

_____

_____

_____

_____

_____

_____

_____

_____

_____

_____

_____

_____

_____

Reflection Notes

Date: _____

_____

_____

_____

_____

_____

_____

_____

_____

_____

_____

_____

_____

_____

_____

Made in the USA
Columbia, SC
25 August 2024

41161878R00087